IMAGES
*of America*

# IRVINE

**IRVINE RANCH.** The Santa Ana Valley is home to the Irvine Ranch, which, for many years, was one of the most productive agricultural regions in California. Known for its dramatic contrasts, the oblong ranch is approximately 22 miles long and nine miles wide and runs from the Santa Ana Mountains to the Pacific Ocean. (Used with permission of The Irvine Company. © The Irvine Company LLC 2011. All Rights Reserved.)

**ON THE COVER:** In 1965, Irvine Ranch cowboys became neighbors to the newly opened San Joaquin Golf Course. Cattle operations continued for decades while golfers teed off yards away. The cowboys' days were numbered, however, as ranching soon gave way to residential development. (Used with permission of The Irvine Company. © The Irvine Company LLC 2011. All Rights Reserved.)

IMAGES
*of America*

# IRVINE

Ellen Bell and the
Irvine Historical Society

ARCADIA
PUBLISHING

Published by Arcadia Publishing
Charleston, South Carolina


Library of Congress Control Number: 2011925502

For all general information, please contact Arcadia Publishing:
Telephone 843-853-2070
Fax 843-853-0044
E-mail sales@arcadiapublishing.com
For customer service and orders:
Toll-Free 1-888-313-2665

Visit us on the Internet at www.arcadiapublishing.com

*To Tim, Tyler, and Katie Bell and the Irvine history we've shared together*

IRVINE HISTORICAL MUSEUM. The Irvine Historical Museum building was part of the original Irvine Ranch house. This addition, built in 1877, is the oldest remaining structure on the ranch. The museum is located at 5 San Joaquin in Irvine, California.

# CONTENTS

# ACKNOWLEDGMENTS

The best part about writing a book like this is having the opportunity to meet so many wonderful people along the way. The history of the Irvine Ranch has already been well documented. My job was to learn as much of it as possible and then make the stories come to life with historic images. Fortunately for me, there were dedicated local historians ready to patiently listen to my questions and generously lead me to the answers.

I have lived in the city of Irvine for nearly half of my life and still was not aware of the rich history of my hometown. This journey has caused me to see the landscape of the Irvine Ranch from a new perspective. This book was created in partnership with gifted historian Gail Daniels and the Irvine Historical Society. Mary Susa, Ann Davis Johnson, and many others who volunteer at the Irvine Historical Museum deserve many thanks.

Orange County is fortunate to have excellent research collections available to the public. The following institutions were essential to my project, and I am grateful for their resources and encouragement: Dr. William Hendricks at the Sherman Library, Susan Berumen and Chris Jepsen at the Orange County Archives, Steve MacLeod at the University of California, Irvine Special Collections Library, Jennifer Ring at the Bowers Museum, Bob Blankman at First American Corporation, and Richard Serrato and Nadya Iotova at the Katie Wheeler Library.

I am indebted to many Irvine pioneers who took the time to share their personal recollections with me. Many thanks go to Linda Irvine Smith; Bill White; Bill "Mac" Jeffrey; George Veeh; Hardy Strozier; Dr. Dennis Mull and Dorothy Mull; and Doris, Robert, and Mike Meyers.

Many thanks go as well to Aynsley Clements of the Irvine Company and Tom Macduff from the City of Irvine for providing historic images as soon as I asked for them. Also, thanks are extended to Bob Huttar, of the Irvine Ranch Conservancy, for giving me the "ground truth" about historic sites.

I am especially grateful for the expert advice of historians Judy Gauntt Liebeck and Jim Sleeper, who graciously gave me the benefit of their years of research. Finally, thanks go to Guy Ball, Terry Magee, Betty Krogstad, Nicole Nelson, Ben Peters, and Barbara DeMarco-Barrett, who sustained me with their sage advice and much appreciated kindness.

Unless otherwise noted, all images used in this book come from the Irvine Historical Museum collection.

# INTRODUCTION

It may seem that the relatively young city of Irvine has little history to share, but the community of today can trace its roots back hundreds of years, to a time when the land was a vast, sprawling ranch populated with more cattle than people. Over the years, Irvine has been transformed. What was once a pastoral, rural landscape has become a vibrant community with more than 200,000 citizens.

All through its history, people have shaped the transformation of Irvine. Whether it was the Native American Gabrielinos, the flamboyant dons of the rancho era, or the determined members of a first-generation Irish American family, the fingerprints of former residents are everywhere. The street names tell the story—Portolá, Culver, Michelson, Jeffrey, and Jamboree. Everywhere you look in the modern city of Irvine, there are markers from its past.

Irvine has always reaped the benefits of sound planning. James H. Irvine saw great potential in the land that he inherited in 1895. Over his 55 years as owner of the Irvine Ranch, the 100,000-acre landholding went from undeveloped grazing pastures to one of the premier agricultural producers in the world. It did not happen by accident. Irvine meticulously managed his ranch, watching over every aspect of its operation and planning for the future by developing a dependable water supply.

But even a planner like Irvine could not have foreseen the future of his ranch. After World War II, a tidal wave of residential development spread across Southern California, and the Irvine Ranch was directly in its path. But, instead of ceding to the pressures of growth and selling off land in pieces, the Irvine Company had a better plan.

The result was a master-planned community, a revolutionary concept at the time. The wide-open space of the Irvine Ranch provided a blank canvas for city planners and architects. Families flocked to the young city in droves, creating a vital community spirit. Due to the unique luxury of space, Irvine has been able to grow intentionally, taking the time for each new neighborhood to take root and develop. Decades after its incorporation, the master plan of Irvine is still coming to fruition.

Today, Irvine is one of the most desirable communities in Orange County. The public schools are rated among the best in the state, and the city has been honored as "America's Safest City" multiple times. It is home to an industrial-business complex and a university that are envied worldwide. But these achievements did not happen overnight—Irvine's present-day success can be directly traced to the vision and commitment of the people from its past. It was all part of the plan.

"Good news! I've just unloaded the whole rancho on a tenderfoot named Irvine!"

ORANGE COUNTY ILLUSTRATED MAGAZINE, 1961. Political cartoonist Burr Shafer pokes fun at local history by putting his own satirical spin on the acquisition of Irvine Ranch land from the Californios. This cartoon was published during Irvine's transition from an agricultural center to a residential, planned community. (Courtesy Orange County Archives.)

# *One*

# RANCHO DAYS

In the beginning, there was land: an open expanse of rolling hills and fertile lowlands stretching from the mountains to the sea. The Irvine area's native people were of Shoshonean origin and called either Gabrielinos or Juanenos, depending on mission affiliation. They lived off the land, using reeds from local marshlands to build shelters and weave elaborate baskets. They were peaceful people who believed that their god, Chinigchinich, watched over them from high on Saddleback Mountain.

Their story changed in 1769, when the king of Spain decided to establish more permanent colonies in California and sent Capt. Gaspar de Portolá to find suitable mission sites. When de Portolá's party camped near the Santa Ana River, it experienced a terrifying earthquake. The padres named it Nombre Dulce de Jesus De Los Temblores, or Sweet Name of Jesus of the Earthquakes. The soldiers opted for a shorter title—El Rio de Santa Ana, named for St. Anne. Mission San Juan Capistrano, established in 1776, flourished under Spanish rule. However, in 1833, the newly independent Mexican government secularized the missions, forcing them to surrender their vast landholdings. Within a few years, the once powerful missions fell into decline.

Mexican land grants were issued to the patriarchs of influential families, dividing the land into feudal estates. The Gabrielino Indians became cowboys, or vaqueros, and learned to manage cattle on horseback. The rancho era is one of the most romanticized periods of California history, and no one personified the age more than Don Jose Andres Sepulveda, of the Rancho San Joaquin. An excellent horseman with a penchant for lavish living, Sepulveda became one of the richest men in California by selling beef to hungry miners during the Gold Rush. He and his large family hosted rodeos, bullfights, and fiestas at his adobe, named El Refugio. But when devastating drought and years of extravagance finally caught up with Sepulveda in 1864, the mounting debt forced him to sell his rancho to the sheep-grazing operation of Flint, Bixby and Company; "and Company" referred to a silent partner named James Irvine.

**MISSION INDIAN SHELTER.** The Tongva (Gabrielino) and Acjachemem (Juaneño) people lived off what the land had to offer. Seeds, berries, and local wildlife were their primary food supply. Their shelters were primitive huts called *kiicha*, which were made from reeds and marshland grasses. When a *kiicha* became damaged or infested, its occupants would simply burn it and build another. (Courtesy O'Neill Museum.)

Gaspar de Portola

**CAPT. GASPAR DE PORTOLÁ (1716–1784).** In 1769, De Portolá led an expedition of 66 soldiers and padres in search of suitable mission sites north of San Diego. The party camped at a natural spring at the base of the Santa Ana foothills that was later named Tomato Springs for the wild tomatoes that grew there. Today, Portolá's spring is located below the 241 Toll Road, north of the former El Toro Marine Base.

MISSION SAN JUAN CAPISTRANO
FOUNDED 1776
DESTROYED BY EARTHQUAKE 1812

**MISSION SAN JUAN CAPISTRANO, BEFORE 1812 EARTHQUAKE.** After the founding of the Mission San Juan Capistrano in 1776, much of the land that now makes up Irvine was considered part of mission territory and used for grazing the mission's sizeable herd of cattle. (Courtesy O'Neill Museum.)

**HENRI PENELON'S DON BERNARDO YORBA, C. 1840.** The Yorba family received one of the first land grants in the Santa Ana Valley—62,000 acres on the east bank of the Santa Ana River, called the Rancho Santiago de Santa Ana. By 1846, Don Bernardo Yorba (1800–1858) was the head of the family. On the other side of the river, his brother Teodocio owned the Rancho Lomas de Santiago. Portions of both ranchos later became the Irvine Ranch. (Courtesy Bowers Museum, Santa Ana, California.)

11

**DON JOSE ANDRES SEPULVEDA (1801–1875).** Sepulveda epitomized the larger-than-life ranchero. It is believed that he had so many horses on his Rancho San Joaquin that he kept them in several corrals, separated by color. His legendary equestrian skills were only surpassed by his flair for fashionable clothing. Even though Sepulveda could only sign documents with an X, he managed to send two of his sons to Harvard for formal educations.

**JAMES WALKER'S VAQUEROS AT ROUNDUP.** The cattle of the rancho period were longhorns, a leaner, more self-sufficient breed that could graze independently. Known as "California Dollars," longhorns were not raised for their beef, but for their hides, which were shipped to the New England leather shoe industry, and for their tallow, which was used to make soap and candles. (Courtesy First American Corporation.)

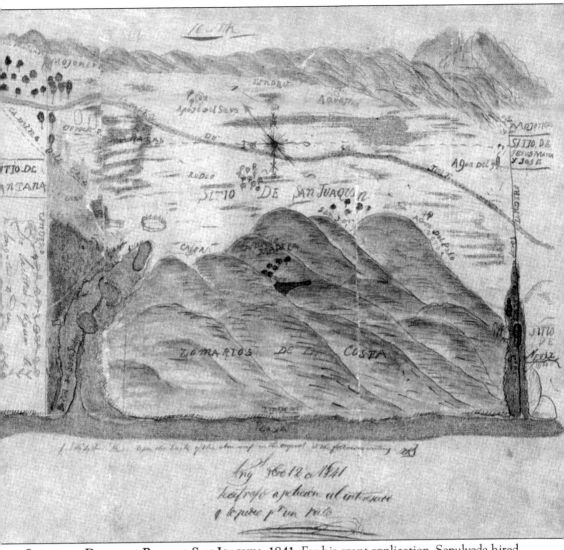

**SEPULVEDA DISENO OF RANCHO SAN JOAQUIN, 1841.** For his grant application, Sepulveda hired William Money to create a map that used natural landmarks and existing structures to mark its borders. Sepulveda's request for land was granted. His Rancho San Joaquin ran from Red Hill to Newport Bay, then south to Laguna Canyon, and later made up the lower half of the Irvine Ranch, including the current cities of Newport Beach, Tustin, and Laguna Beach. (Courtesy Sherman Library.)

**SWAMP OF THE FROGS.** Runoff from the Santa Ana foothills drained down into the lowlands, creating a waterlogged marshland. The swamp covered the Back Bay area and extended to Red Hill, in present-day Tustin. Californios named it Cienega de los Ranas, or "Swamp of the Frogs," because of the tremendous croaking noise of the tree frogs that lived in the marsh. The song of the frogs was so loud that it served as an audible landmark to travelers even in the dark of night.

**BEAR AND BULL FIGHTS.** Since entertainment was scarce, rancheros staged fights between their bulls and captured grizzly bears from the local foothills. Pioneer J.E. Pleasants, who witnessed such fights on the San Joaquin, wrote, "There was nothing tame about them." His account in the *San Joaquin Gazette* states that if the bull won, he lived to graze another day. But no victorious grizzly was ever rewarded with its freedom. After killing one of Don Jose Sepulveda's prized bulls, the bear paid the ultimate penalty of death.

HENRI PENELON'S *DON JOSE SEPULVEDA*, C. **1856.** On March 21, 1852, Don Jose Sepulveda challenged Pio Pico's unbeaten horse, Sarco, to a race. Sepulveda's horse was a newcomer to the area, an Australian mare named Black Swan. The wager of cash and cattle was staggering for both men, who literally bet their fortunes on a single race. News of the event spread like wildfire, and people came to Los Angeles from all over to witness the nine-mile race. A lightweight boy rode Black Swan on an English saddle, while Sarco's larger rider used a traditional heavy vaquero saddle. The race was a battle, but in the end Black Swan and Sepulveda were victorious. Victory for the horse was short-lived, however, as the champion mare died of lockjaw within a year. (Courtesy Bowers Museum, Santa Ana, California.)

**THE PURSUIT OF JUAN FLORES, 1857.** In the 1850s, life on the ranchos exemplified the Wild West, with stagecoach robberies and gangs of bandits who terrorized settlers. One of the most notorious bandits in 1857 was Juan Flores, who, along with his gang, had descended upon the village of San Juan Capistrano. Word was sent to Los Angeles, where Sheriff James Barton and five deputies set out to apprehend the bandits. Barton and his men spent the night at the Sepulveda adobe on the Rancho San Joaquin, where Don Jose advised them not to fight Flores with so few men. Sheriff Barton ignored the warning and continued in the morning. On the way to Capistrano, Barton and three of his men were ambushed and murdered on a hill that would later bear his name. Today, Barton's Mound is located on the southeast corner of the 405 Freeway interchange with the Laguna Freeway.

**ANDRES PICO (1810–1876).** James Barton was the first sheriff killed in the line of duty in the state of California. After Barton's murder, Gen. Andres Pico formed a larger posse. For the first time, both Americans and Californios joined together in the search for Juan Flores. Flores and his gang were pursued into the foothills, where Flores eluded capture by jumping off a peak near Modjeska Canyon. He was captured one day later and held overnight at Yorba's adobe.

**HANGMAN'S TREE.** During the night, Juan Flores escaped. When General Pico heard the news, he took two captured gang members and hanged them on a nearby tree. Days later, Juan Flores was captured in the Simi Pass and was hanged in a public execution in Los Angeles. The Hangman's Tree, pictured here with historian Chris Jepsen, still stands in the Irvine Ranch Conservancy about 100 yards from the 241 Toll Road. (Courtesy Chris Jepsen.)

**WILLIAM WOLFSKILL (1798–1866).** Wolfskill was a pioneer in the Southern California citrus industry and is credited with creating the Valencia orange hybrid. In 1860, he purchased the Rancho Lomas de Santiago from Teodosio Yorba. Six years later, he sold the land, as well as his Valencia hybrid, to Flint, Bixby and Company for $7,000. The 47,000-acre parcel became the northern half of the Irvine Ranch, giving its owners water rights to the Santa Ana River. (Courtesy Joan Hedding.)

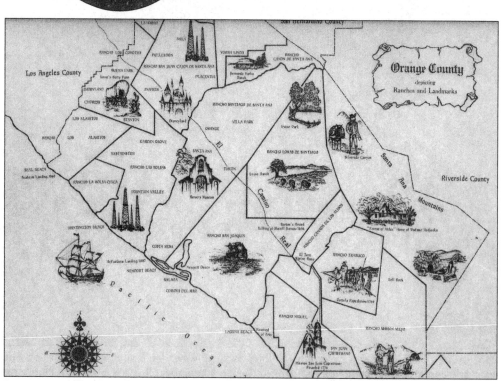

**RANCHOS OF ORANGE COUNTY.** The Irvine Ranch was made up of portions of three large Spanish Mexican land grants: the Rancho Santiago de Santa Ana, the Rancho Lomas de Santiago, and the Rancho San Joaquin. Altogether, the new Irvine Ranch consisted of over 110,000 acres.

# Two

# THE DAWN OF THE IRVINE RANCH

*"I tell you a boy cast upon the world without a dollar in his pocket*
*. . . can appreciate the value of a helping hand."*

—James Irvine,
as quoted in R. Glass Cleland's *The Irvine Ranch*

At the age of 19, James Irvine left Belfast, Ireland, to seek success in America. After a brief stint in a New York paper mill, he was lured to California by tales of the gold rush. Irvine's journey was long and arduous, culminating in a fateful, 102-day voyage to San Francisco. While on board the Dutch ship *Alexander Humboldt*, he met two men who would have a lasting impact on his life—one became an archenemy, the other a valuable business partner. During the voyage, Irvine clashed with future railroad giant Collis P. Huntington. Irvine never forgot the slight, which led to a confrontation years later. Another shipboard relationship was more fruitful, when Irvine met Benjamin Flint, a land speculator and wool merchant, whose partnership would lead Irvine to his future ranch.

Young James Irvine struck it rich in San Francisco, but not as a gold-miner. He became a successful merchant, supplying food and provisions to the men in the mines. A shrewd investor, Irvine parlayed his profits into revenue-generating property in the boomtown of San Francisco. At 37, Irvine was rich and ready for his next challenge. His old friend Benjamin Flint provided the opportunity.

The Civil War had disrupted cotton production, so Flint decided to meet the demand with wool. Together with his brother Thomas and his cousin Llewellyn Bixby, Flint purchased land in Monterey County for the purpose of grazing sheep. Irvine became an investor in Flint, Bixby and Company, and soon the successful partners began to look for more grazing lands in Southern California. There, they found cash-strapped rancheros desperate to sell. In 1864, Irvine and his partners paid three bits an acre, or roughly $41,000, for 168 square miles of future Orange County landscape. Twelve years later, Irvine bought out his partners for $150,000, and the Irvine Ranch was born.

Irvine experienced a dramatic change of fortune during his lifetime. At the time of his death, in 1886, the scrappy Irish immigrant who arrived in this country without a dollar in his pocket had amassed a fortune valued at well over one million dollars.

**JAMES IRVINE AS A BOY.** According to James Felton's *The Irvines: A Family Portrait*, Irvine was born in Ireland in 1827, but he celebrated his Scottish ancestry. He described himself as "the son of a farmer in easy circumstance." One of nine children, Irvine was a "good diligent student whose great powers of analysis found stimulus in mathematics." No doubt the virtues of disciplined living were instilled in the boy. Irvine's favorite maxims, kept in the family Bible, were "Ever live within your income" and "Keep good company or none." (Used with permission of The Irvine Company. © The Irvine Company LLC 2011. All Rights Reserved.)

**VOYAGE ON THE *HUMBOLDT*, 1849.** James Irvine's journey to San Francisco was not an easy one. First, he sailed from New York to the east coast of Panama. Then, in the days before the Panama Canal, Irvine had to cross the isthmus on mule, by canoe, and on foot. According to historian Judy Liebeck, he boarded the Dutch ship *Alexander Humboldt* for a 102-day voyage, on which he endured "hard beans and hardtack, mahogany beef and bilge water daily."

**SAN FRANCISCO, 1850.** San Francisco was a boomtown when Irvine arrived in 1849. Six years later, he joined a relative in a successful business named Irvine & Co., Wholesale Produce and Grocery Merchants. Irvine then parlayed his profits into real estate. By 1870, his San Francisco properties were valued at $200,000.

21

**James Irvine and Henrietta "Nettie" Rice, 1866.** Irvine had become a prominent citizen in San Francisco and, since his parents had immigrated to Cleveland, Ohio, he was also familiar with that city. There, he met Henrietta Maria "Nettie" Rice (1841–1874), whom he married in 1866. Irvine brought his bride to San Francisco, where they bought a home at Folsom and Eleventh Streets. Their happiness grew in 1867, when Nettie gave birth to their first son, James Harvey Irvine, on October 16. Nettie contracted puerperal fever soon after childbirth, and for days Irvine feared he would lose his wife. After the crisis passed, he wrote to his in-laws, "I am going to do all in my power to benefit or make her happy; I love her too dearly to do otherwise."

**HARVEY RICE (1800–1891).** Nettie Rice came from a distinguished family. Her father, Harvey Rice, was an educator, author, and pioneering political leader in the state of Ohio. Since he sponsored the bill that established the first public school and libraries in the state, he was known as the "father of the common school system of Ohio." (Courtesy Katie Wheeler Library.)

**SHEEP-RAISING INVESTMENT.** In 1853, Flint, Bixby and Company brought 2,000 head of sheep from Iowa to Monterey County, California, where it had purchased 50,000 acres of land for grazing. To fund this venture, Benjamin Flint turned to his old shipmate, James Irvine, who provided capital as a silent partner. The investment was profitable, and Flint, Bixby and Company looked for more land farther south, below Los Angeles. (Courtesy City of Irvine.)

23

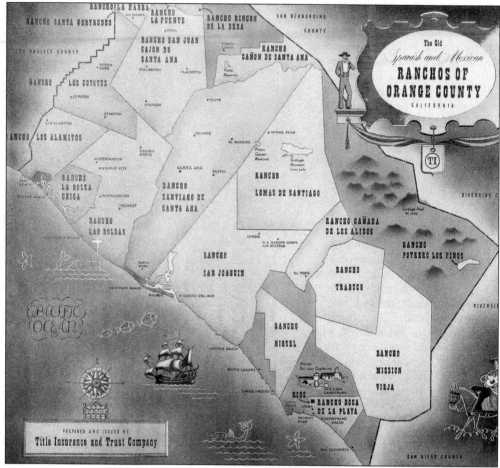

The map shows "The Old Spanish and Mexican RANCHOS OF ORANGE COUNTY CALIFORNIA" with various ranchos labeled including Rancho La Habra, Rancho Santa Gertrudes, Rancho La Puente, Rancho Rincon De La Brea, Rancho San Juan Cajon De Santa Ana, Rancho Cañon De Santa Ana, Rancho Los Coyotes, Rancho Los Alamitos, Rancho La Bolsa Chica, Rancho Las Bolsas, Rancho Santiago De Santa Ana, Rancho Lomas De Santiago, Rancho Cañada De Los Alisos, Rancho Potrero Los Pinos, Rancho San Joaquin, Rancho Trabuco, Rancho Niguel, Rancho Mission Vieja, Rancho Boca De La Playa. Prepared and issued by Title Insurance and Trust Company.

**THE IRVINE RANCH.** Conditions in the Santa Ana Valley were ripe for Flint, Bixby and Company. The Great Drought of 1862–1864 had wiped out the local cattle, leaving the rancheros destitute and desperate. Plus, the legal cost of defending their land claims to the new American government had forced them to mortgage their properties. Unable to pay, the rancheros were forced to sell, and the Flint brothers, Bixby, and Irvine were ready to make an offer. In 1864, they purchased portions of three Spanish Mexican land grants. (Courtesy First American Corporation.)

**VAST LANDHOLDING.** Irvine visited his newly purchased land in the summer of 1867 and was pleased with what he saw. "We rode about a great deal," he wrote, "sometimes coming home in the evening after a thirty or forty mile ride, pretty thoroughly tired out, but we had to do it to see much of the ranch and the flock."

24

**FIRST RANCH HOUSE.** In 1868, Irvine had a ranch house built in order to have a suitable place to stay during his visits. The two-story house was the finest for miles and was the first wooden structure built between Anaheim and San Diego. The addition on the left side of the house was built in 1877 and is currently the home of the Irvine Historical Museum.

**SHEEP BARN AT ORIGINAL RANCH HOUSE.** Charles E. French was hired as ranch superintendent in 1870, but the conditions on the sheep ranch made the former Bostonian soon regret his decision. The only way to get rid of the fleas was to flood the house. Historian Liebeck writes that French "flooded the floors and plastered the walls to get rid of these pests." At night, he had to "jump into bed as quickly as possible in order to not get them in bed."

**Sheepshearing on the San Joaquin.** In 1867, Irvine imported 25 thoroughbred Spanish merino sheep in order to improve the quality of the wool. Irvine's father-in-law, Harvey Rice, writes in his book *Letters from the Pacific Slope*: "the annual clip of wool from the sheep of this ranch is said to be about 200,000 pounds of the finest quality. It is easy to see that wool-growing is a very profitable business in California." By the end of 1868, the ranch was stocked with 45,000 sheep. (Courtesy O'Neill Museum.)

**First Farm Buildings at Irvine Ranch.** In 1875, C.E. French wrote to James Irvine asking for permission to "do a little farming on his own responsibility and at his own risk." Irvine agreed, but stated that "it could not be any expense to the ranch." French was successful at growing "dry crops" of wheat and barley. Irvine was pleased and told French to allow parts of the ranch to be used for tenant farming, providing the tenants assumed full responsibility.

**JAMES IRVINE, C. 1870.** The year 1874 was a tragic one for Irvine. His second son, Harvey Rice Irvine, died in infancy, and his beloved wife, Nettie, died months later of tuberculosis. His first son, James Harvey Irvine, was only seven years old. Years later, in 1880, Irvine married Margaret Byrne in San Francisco. Although 1876 was a year of devastating drought, Irvine's love for his land did not diminish. In September of that year, he bought out his partners for $150,000 and became the sole owner of what could now be called the Irvine Ranch. Even though Irvine now owned one-fifth of what was about to become Orange County, he remained an absentee landowner, residing primarily in San Francisco with his young son.

**IRVINE FAMILY HOME.** After years of living at the isolated ranch house, French's wife, Emma, longed for a home closer to civilization. In 1876, the Frenches moved to Santa Ana and began to look for a new location for the Irvine home and ranch headquarters. French settled on an area close to the Tustin City stagecoach line, and construction on the Irvine Ranch house began soon after. (Courtesy Katie Wheeler Library.)

**MADAME HELENA MODJESKA (1840–1909).** Polish Shakespearean actress Madame Helena Modjeska was one of the most famous women of her time. She came to the Santiago Canyon in 1876 and built a rustic retreat that she named Arden. Both Modjeska Canyon and Modjeska Peak, on Saddleback Mountain, were named in her honor. Modjeska became a close personal friend of the Irvine family.

**STAGECOACH LINE.** The Seeley-Wright Stagecoach Company operated a line through the Irvine Ranch in the 1870s. Passengers from San Diego were promised to reach Los Angeles in 24 hours. The stage drivers followed the El Camino Real, staying close to the foothills and keeping watch for bandits. If the stagecoach made it across the Irvine Ranch safely, the driver would stop for fresh horses at the Adobe Station, located at Bryan and Browning Avenues in Tustin, before heading on to Los Angeles.

**COLLIS P. HUNTINGTON (1821–1900).** The arrival of the railroad signaled the end of the stagecoach era. The Southern Pacific Line and its owner, Collis P. Huntington, wanted to extend railroad service to San Diego, but the Irvine Ranch was in the way. Irvine was not about to yield to the man who had offended him 25 years earlier, on the ship to San Francisco. Huntington sued Irvine in federal court, but Irvine won the lawsuit, stopping the Southern Pacific in its tracks.

**SOUTHERN PACIFIC CONFRONTATION, 1887.** Even though Irvine had won the first battle with the Southern Pacific Railroad, the war was not over. After Irvine's death, the Southern Pacific tried to cross the ranch again, this time without permission. On a Saturday afternoon, when the courts were closed for the weekend, the railroad crew began to lay tracks through Tustin and onto the Irvine Ranch. There, they were met by George Irvine, James's brother, who was trustee of the ranch. He and a crew of armed ranch hands promptly ran the railroad crew off the ranch. Even after death, Irvine won the battle over his old nemesis Huntington. The Southern Pacific Railroad was never allowed access across the Irvine Ranch. Instead, an agreement was made with a rival railroad, the Santa Fe, on April 25, 1887.

**JAMES IRVINE DIES, 1886.** After suffering with a kidney ailment known as Bright's disease, Irvine (pictured at right) died in 1886. He left his estate to his wife, Margaret, and to his 18-year-old son, James Harvey (below), who would inherit the Irvine Ranch on his 25th birthday. Until that time, James Harvey's uncle, George Irvine, and a group of advisors acted as trustees of the estate. A mere 13 months after Irvine's death, the trustees put the ranch up for sale at public auction. Historian Robert Glass Cleland writes, "In the hectic moments of the sale, the official timekeeper became momentarily confused and it was unclear who had offered the successful bid." Since no clear winner was declared, the sale was cancelled, and the Irvine Ranch stayed under family control.

MULE POWER, C. 1890. The new County of Orange was created in 1888. Railroad lines made farming profitable, and more ranch operations were converted from grazing to agriculture. Over 5,000 acres of Irvine Ranch land had been leased, at a rate of 62.5¢ per acre, to farmers who raised hay and grain. Large mule teams were used to pull the threshing machines during harvest. (Courtesy First American Corporation.)

BICYCLE JOURNEY, 1888. In 1888, 21-year-old James Harvey Irvine (left?) and his friend, Harry Bechtel, ride their high-wheeled velocipedes on a three-month journey from San Francisco to San Diego. Along the way, Irvine was able to survey the Irvine Ranch from a new perspective, enjoying the beauty of the land that would soon become his lifelong passion.

# *Three*

# DIVERSIFYING FROM SHEEP TO BEANS

The late 1800s were pioneering days in California, and no one embodied that spirit more than James Harvey Irvine. Not a typical child of privilege, Irvine was a reflection of his time. He was serious and determined and believed in the ability of every man to make his own way in the world. Instead of observing life from the lofty distance of advantages and wealth, Irvine preferred to experience things firsthand, choosing to ground himself in the natural world.

At the time of his inheritance, the only asset of the underdeveloped Irvine Ranch was its potential. But under the careful stewardship of Irvine, known to his friends as J.I., the land was transformed from a sleepy sheep-grazing operation into an agricultural powerhouse.

Irvine inherited his father's shrewd business acumen and his formidable self-discipline. He was a man of few words, preferring to let his actions speak for him. His critics said he was aloof, distant, and unemotional. Those who knew him best defended his reticence as the defense mechanism of a wealthy and powerful man. They also spoke of his tremendous personal loss and the natural shyness that caused him to guard his emotions in public. Irvine did not suffer fools easily and detested social niceties as a waste of time. But he was a man of his word, fiercely loyal to his family, and generous with those in need.

Like his contemporary, Theodore Roosevelt, Irvine was a man of action who preferred to "speak softly and carry a big stick." He was a progressive thinker, interested in scientific innovation and the latest technological advances of his time. But he also believed in responsible land management, conservation, and the benefits of exploring the great outdoors. It was this passionate regard for the land, and his determination to keep it intact, that made the present-day city of Irvine possible.

JAMES H. IRVINE, C. 1890. Even though the trustees had tried to auction off the ranch before he could inherit it, young James Harvey Irvine was anxious to begin his tenure as landowner. James Felton writes that Irvine said later, "It was lucky for my side young as I was, I wanted the ranch." (Courtesy First American Corporation.)

ENTRY GATES TO IRVINE FAMILY HOME. Until 1892, the ranch was under the care of resident trustee George Irvine, who made significant improvements to the property. "Uncle George" supervised the construction of the wide, private road extending from Tustin City to the family home, later called Irvine Boulevard. The wrought iron entry gates, from San Francisco, were added in 1891, and the Washingtonian palm trees were planted in 1906. (Courtesy First American Corporation.)

BLACKSMITH SHOP, 1910. One of the earliest structures at the ranch headquarters was the blacksmith shop, which was built in 1888. It was later expanded to fit the needs of the growing ranch operations. A carriage barn was added in 1895 to house and feed the all-important mules, and a home was built for ranch manager C.F. Krauss in 1897. The latter two structures are still standing at the Irvine Ranch Historic Park. (Courtesy Katie Wheeler Library.)

FAMILY HOME SCREENED PORCH. Originally, ranch staff ate in the family dining room and workers ate on a screened porch on the south end of the home. George Irvine conducted business from an office off the entrance hall. In 1891, a separate office building was built facing the home's driveway. (Courtesy Katie Wheeler Library.)

**TENANT FARMERS.** The fenceless property of the Irvine Ranch was constantly at the mercy of homesteaders trying to gain a piece of the land for themselves. To solve the problem, George Irvine encouraged tenant farmers to sharecrop in order to keep the land productive and discourage squatters.

**JEFFREY LIMA BEAN FIELD, 1911.** The Jeffrey family began farming on the Irvine Ranch in 1897, first growing lima beans and grain and then Valencia oranges. George Jeffrey served as Orange County supervisor from 1922 to 1934 and planned the area's first paved road system. Jeffrey Road was named to honor George and the generations of his family that lived and worked on the Irvine Ranch. (Courtesy Bowers Museum, Santa Ana, California.)

**JAMES H. IRVINE AND FRANCES ANITA PLUM, C. 1895.** 1892 was an important year for James Irvine. Not only did he inherit the Irvine Ranch on his 25th birthday, but he also married San Francisco socialite Frances Anita Plum. According to James P. Felton of the Newport Beach Historical Society, Irvine was described as a "tall, rather shy, retiring young man, who has plenty of business capacity to care for the million odd his father left him." (Courtesy Katie Wheeler Library.)

**IRVINE CHILDREN, C. 1899.** The Irvine family grew quickly. Their first child, James Harvey Jr., known as "Jase," was born on June 11, 1893. He was soon followed by sister Kathryn Helena, named for family friend Madame Helena Modjeska, on April 25, 1894. Four years later, a second son, Myford Plum, completed the family. (Courtesy Katie Wheeler Library.)

**IRVINE COMPANY SEAL.** While on his honeymoon, Irvine heard about the benefits of incorporating in West Virginia due to the state's business-friendly laws. He followed the advice and, in 1894, formed the Irvine Company. J.I. was the only stockholder until his death, 53 years later.

**IRVINE RANCH CATTLE BRAND, 1892.** Ranchers were required to submit their specific cattle brand to the Orange County assessor's office. When J.I. inherited the ranch, this leather brand sample was filed. The sample also indicates that Irvine cattle would have specific notches in the ear; the left markings were for the heifers and the right markings were for the steer. (Courtesy Orange County Archives.)

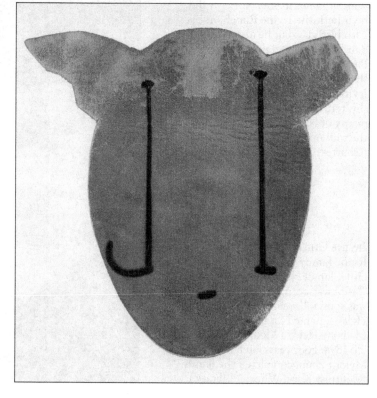

**JASE AND KATHRYN IRVINE AT PICNIC GROUNDS, 1896.** Irvine loved the wide expanses of his ranch, especially a grove of ancient oak trees near Santiago Creek. For years, pioneers had been coming to the spot they called "the Picnic Grounds." It was Irvine's favorite retreat, and he enjoyed bringing his young family there and passing on his love of nature to his children. (Courtesy Katie Wheeler Library.)

**ORANGE COUNTY PARK.** In 1897, Irvine gave 160 acres of the northern portion of his ranch to Orange County. He wished to create a regional park in order to preserve the natural beauty of the ancient trees that grew there. The park became a local treasure and thousands of county residents enjoyed festive annual picnics and concerts on the grounds. On June 1, 1926, Orange County passed a resolution to change its name to Irvine Regional Park.

PETERS CANYON RESERVOIR. In the early 1890s, production was limited to dry-crop farming, such as barley. In 1892, Irvine decided to experiment with the cultivation of lima beans. He knew that a dependable water supply would be crucial. In 1893, he exercised his water rights to the Santa Ana River and began diverting water from Santiago Creek, its largest tributary. The water then filled Peters Canyon Reservoir for use on the Irvine Ranch.

IRRIGATION PIPELINE. In order to raise the money for irrigation on the ranch, Irvine sold coastline land parcels in Newport Beach and Laguna Beach. Irvine asked friends at the Standard Oil Company to dig 14 deepwater wells, each powered by gasoline engine pumps. Over the next 11 years, 44 wells were dug—many to a depth of 1,200 feet. In 1910, the Irvine Company laid about 50,000 feet of concrete pipeline, finally establishing a dependable water supply. (Courtesy Bowers Museum, Santa Ana, California.)

**Newmark and Edwards Warehouse, Built in 1889.** Before the railroad came to the Irvine Ranch in 1887, all crops were processed and shipped through Tustin warehouses. George Irvine decided to take advantage of the new rail line on his land and commissioned his own warehouse in 1889. Builders Newmark and Edwards constructed a barley warehouse on a site that was 130 feet above sea level, the highest point on the Irvine Ranch.

**First Post Office.** Soon after the warehouse was constructed, a home was built for the family of the town cook. The Paschall family lived in the house, which functioned as a small dining hall for workers and a boardinghouse for local schoolteachers. Eventually, in 1899, it became the first post office.

**IRVINE FAMILY HOME ON PAGE STREET IN SAN FRANCISCO.** When the San Francisco earthquake struck in 1906, Irvine was on the ranch and away from his family. Unable to confirm their safety, he took the first available northbound train. Fortunately, he found Frances and the children unharmed. Irvine vowed never to be separated from his family again. The entire family relocated to live at the ranch full-time.

**IRVINE RANCH HOUSE, 1908.** With his family now living on the ranch, J.I. expanded the home, nearly doubling its original size. By 1908, the two-story Georgian country house had become a 30-room residence. By all accounts, the Irvine home, known by the family as the "ranch house," was comfortable, with plenty of room for the children and Irvine's hunting dogs to play. (Courtesy Katie Wheeler Library.)

IRVINE FAMILY HOME INTERIOR, 1908. Irvine's practical nature would not allow for an ostentatious household. For years, there was no central heating system. Historian Jim Sleeper recounts that when asked why he did not install one as a kindness for his guests, Irvine responded, "If they're cold, let 'em wear these things," revealing a pair of timeworn long underwear. (Courtesy Katie Wheeler Library.)

IRVINE FAMILY ON PORCH, 1908. The family's first years at the Irvine Ranch were happy ones, even if they were few in number. Pictured here, from left to right, are Frances Irvine, her son Jase, her daughter Kathryn, and two unidentified people. Frances was pleased to have her family together under one roof. But within three short years of their arrival, personal tragedy would change the Irvine family forever.

**FREDERICK AND AGNES CULVER.** In 1902, tenant farmer Frederick Culver planted lima beans and became one of the most successful farmers in Orange County. One of the smallest men on the ranch, Culver was a hunchback who appeared to be deceptively frail. But the man they called "Humpy" was respected as a good businessman and an even better man. When he died, he left a sizeable estate to his wife, Agnes, and his daughter, Mabel.

**CULVER'S CORNER.** Culver's home, known as "Culver's Corner," was located at the intersection of the 101 (now 5) Freeway, Culver Drive, and Trabuco Road. A 1910 article in the *Daily Evening Blade* states that Culver spared no expense in building the house, which was filled with "all the modern conveniences," including "acetylene gas lighting and a furnace that heats the house throughout." The house sat at one of the deadliest intersections in the county. Culver's wife, Agnes, regularly treated crash victims until they could be transferred to the hospital.

**HARVEST TIME.** Each tenant farmer agreed to provide seed and cultivate the land, giving Irvine a percentage of the crop in return. The Irvine Company advanced money to the farmers and carried the loan, if necessary, from one season to the next. The one-year leases gave Irvine the ability to remove an unsatisfactory tenant, but in most cases leases continued year after year, with many passed from father to son.

**HARVESTING BEANS, 1910.** Beans, mainly lima and black-eyed varieties, were the ideal crop for the parched soil of the Irvine Ranch. Irvine explained in a letter to a fellow farmer: "lima beans take more or less moisture from the atmosphere and do well along the coast of Southern California." The crop was harvested in the fall, and sheep would graze the land clean before it was replanted in May. (Courtesy First American Corporation.)

**THRESHING OPERATION, 1913.** When a farmer was ready to harvest a bean crop, he brought his crop to a threshing outfit, which included a large staff of hired hands and a chuck wagon to feed them all, to come out to his field. After the vines were cut and dried in the fields, they were loaded by pitchfork into net-lined wagons and taken by mule to the stationary thresher. Then, the full

**COOK AND CALLEN'S BEAN-THRESHING OUTFIT.** Since most bean farmers could not afford their own machinery, they relied on threshing outfits like the one operated by George Cook. One of the most successful farmers on the Irvine Ranch, Cook farmed the largest lima bean lease on the ranch. His 17,000-acre lima bean field later became the El Toro Marine Base.

nets were taken out of the wagons and dumped into the threshing machine, which separated the beans from the vines. The beans were loaded into burlap sacks, weighing 100 pounds when filled, that were sewn shut and stacked in the field. Once the harvesting began, the workers stayed out in the fields until they were done—usually in about six weeks.

MODERNIZED BEAN-THRESHING EQUIPMENT. Eventually, the tractor replaced the mule, and gasoline engines replaced steam power. The threshing outfit was now able to come to the farmer's field and harvest on-site, allowing a more efficient way to bring in the bean crop. (Courtesy Bowers Museum, Santa Ana, California.).

**BRINGING CROPS TO THE WAREHOUSE.** After harvest, the bean sacks were loaded onto wagons and brought to the warehouse for cleaning and storage. The heavy sacks were stacked to the ceiling in interlocking piles so as not to fall over, and later unstacked and taken to the shipping area. During the labor-intensive days before bulk processing, the warehouse was open 24 hours a day to get the crops ready for shipping.

**WAGONS WAIT THEIR TURNS TO UNLOAD.** Harvest time meant long lines at the warehouse. Many farmers would set out in the middle of the night to get a place in line. Since every sack was unloaded by hand, the wait could last for hours. In 1895, another warehouse was built that could store up to 200,000 sacks of beans or barley. This structure has been preserved and still stands in Old Town Irvine.

**FIRST SCHOOL, 1906.** By the end of the 19th century, the population of families on the Irvine Ranch had grown enough to merit a school for tenants' children. In 1899, Irvine built a one-room schoolhouse across the railroad tracks from the first warehouse. Average attendance was 80 children; many of them came to school barefoot. (Courtesy Orange County Archives.)

**WAGONS CROSSING CENTRAL AVENUE.** During the fall, the warehouse was the center of activity on the Irvine Ranch. The locals called it "Beantown," even though the official town name was Myford, after Irvine's youngest child. The Irvine School is in the background, facing Central Avenue—appropriately named, because it ran through the center of the little town. The street name was later changed to Sand Canyon Avenue because the road extended to the Sand Canyon Reservoir.

**FRANCES ANITA IRVINE, 1908.** In 1909, on the eve of a trip to Japan with her husband, Frances Anita Irvine died suddenly in San Francisco of a heart attack. A distraught Irvine had to comfort his grieving children, who arrived from the ranch after their mother's death. After 17 years of happy marriage, the irreparable loss of his wife devastated Irvine. Ironically, Madame Helena Modjeska, famed actress and personal friend of Frances Irvine, died the same year.

**JAMES IRVINE ON THE RANCH WITH HUNTING DOG RUFF.** Devastated by the loss of his wife, Irvine retreated to the comfort of his ranch, preferring the company of his hunting dogs. Wherever he went, his Irish setters were not far behind. Irvine was an excellent shot. According to Jim Sleeper, longtime ranch manager Brad Hellis once said, "Mr. Irvine was the best quail shot I ever saw. He could knock out three birds at different angles almost simultaneously." (Courtesy First American Corporation.)

**DUCK HUNTING, 1901.** The Irvine Ranch was a true hunter's paradise. Wild game was so abundant that any marksman with decent aim could bag a prize. There were dozens of gun clubs on the Irvine Ranch, and most were simple and inexpensive. Historian Judy Gauntt writes, "The area around the San Joaquin Duck Club was so full of ducks and geese that when they took wing, they would darken the sky."

**JAMES IRVINE AND PRIZE TUNA CAUGHT ON CATALINA ISLAND, 1899.** Fishing was another passion of Irvine, shown here with his son Jase and a 116-pound tuna. Irvine had the enviable talent of being able to cast two flies at the same time. According to Jim Sleeper, Irvine never took his sportsman's paradise for granted, telling his friend A.J. McFadden, "Mac, you and I are two of the luckiest men in the world. We both love hunting and fishing and we've lived through the golden age of them in California."

IRVINE CHILDREN, C. 1908. The Irvine
children were well adjusted and outgoing,
even after the tragic loss of their mother. Jase
(above right), the eldest, was capable and
well liked, a natural successor to his father.
Kathryn grew to be a beauty. Once, when
pioneering pilot Glenn Martin was trying
to win her affection, he showered the Irvine
family home with flowers from his plane. The
youngest Irvine, Myford (above left), known
as Mike, was softer in personality and more
like his mother than his siblings. He was a
gifted musician who later composed his own
music. (Courtesy Katie Wheeler Library.)

**AERIAL IMAGE OF IRVINE RANCH HEADQUARTERS.** The headquarters compound on Irvine Boulevard was the heart of the Irvine Ranch operation. An island in a sea of citrus and walnut groves, the ranch headquarters housed the workers, the livestock, and even the Irvine family, who lived in the white, Georgian mansion seen in the lower left corner of the image.

**IRVINE OFFICE, BUILT IN 1891.** Even though he owned one-fifth of the county, Irvine felt comfortable in a modest, one-room office near his home. When Brad Hellis came to work at the ranch in 1914, Irvine added an apartment for his new employee. This arrangement remained unchanged until 1929, when a new office building was constructed.

**Mess Hall and Dormitory, Built in 1906.** The expanding ranch workforce created the need for housing. In 1906, a two-story building was constructed with a kitchen and dining room on the first floor and a dormitory upstairs that could house 40 men. The Irvine Ranch could now offer workers a monthly wage of "$30 and board" in a bunkhouse that featured running water and gaslights. Over the years, the bunkhouse kitchen served up ranch-style meals to hungry Irvine Company employees and guests alike.

**Bunkhouse, Built in 1910.** A two-story bunkhouse was added to the compound, close to the Mess Hall. It was used to house the ranch laborers and maintenance men who were not directly involved with work in the fields.

**HOLLY SUGAR COMPANY.** Sugar beets had become a major source of the nation's sugar supply, and the Irvine Ranch was becoming a significant grower. In 1911, the Orange County sugar beet growers formed a cooperative to process their beets into sugar. Irvine donated land and built a factory on Dyer Road. The Holly Sugar Company ran the factory until 1983. Longtime Orange County residents recall passing the factory and holding their noses because of the foul smell.

**LARGEST LIMA BEAN PRODUCTION.** In 1911, Irvine wrote to the *Chicago Produce News*: "We have limas in about 14,000 acres and in black-eyes 4,000 acres . . . forming the largest bean field in the world under one management . . . roughly 180,000 sacks of beans worth about $630,000." During World War I, lima beans became an important food staple for the troops because of their high protein and carbohydrate content and low spoilage rate.

**DEEP WELLS DUG FOR IRRIGATION.** Now that the Irvine Ranch was becoming an established agricultural operation, J.I. invested more capital in his land. In her book *Irvine: A History of Innovation and Growth*, Judy Liebeck writes that Irvine spent between $3 and $4 million to drill 1,200 wells. The wells were powered by electricity from the new Southern California Edison Company.

**WALNUT GROVES.** Long before orange groves covered the Irvine Ranch, walnuts were king. Between 1900 and 1905, the annual walnut harvest was about 22 tons. Before mechanical shakers were available, workers had to harvest walnuts with a long pole and shake the tree. Since the shakers were often looking up into the trees, they regularly faced the hazard of being hit in the face with falling walnuts.

IRVINE STORE AND HOTEL, C. 1915. In 1911, Kate Munger signed a six-month lease to operate a store in the little town of Myford, near the train station. The store was completed one year later and was designed to be the post office as well. In 1913, a hotel was built behind the store to house seasonal workers who came to the ranch during harvest. (Courtesy Orange County Archives.)

IRVINE STORE INTERIOR, C. 1916. The Irvine Store offered local farmers a variety of items, from groceries to hardware. Kate Munger's business was a success, and the store was enlarged within four years. The second story of the building was used as living quarters.

TRAIN DEPOT. When George Irvine agreed to let the Santa Fe Railway have the right-of-way across the ranch in 1887, a "first-class train station" was part of the deal. The station was finally built in 1910. Trains did not routinely stop in Myford; the outgoing mailbag was placed on a hooked post near the track and incoming mail was thrown from the train.

IRVINE, 1915. On May 1, 1914, the town was rechristened "Irvine" when the Northern California town of Irvine changed its name to Carson Hill. This picture, taken from the second floor of the Irvine Store, shows farmers bringing wagonloads to the warehouse and the train depot in the background.

IRVINE SERVICE STATION, C. 1915. Behind the Irvine Store, Kate Munger had a crank-up pump that dispensed Union gasoline, as well as patches for the tube tires. Besides her general store, Munger also farmed a bean lease, tended an apricot grove, and managed a thriving insurance business. (Courtesy Orange County Archives.)

BLACKSMITH SHOP, BUILT IN 1909. Frederick Culver requested permission from James Irvine to build a blacksmith shop near the warehouse. Culver's brother Willard ran the operation, repairing farm machinery, making wagon wheels, and fitting horseshoes. Willard Culver's place in Irvine history was insured when he took part in the most famous local manhunt of the time, the legendary shoot-out with the Tomato Springs Bandit in 1912. From 1928 to 1978, the blacksmith shop was operated by Gene Thomas. Today, the shop building is a restaurant in Old Town Irvine.

**TOMATO SPRINGS BANDIT, 1912.** On a Sunday evening, December 15, 1912, a drifter named Ira Jones attempted to assault a 16-year-old girl at William Cook's bean farm, which later became the El Toro Marine Base. (A) Cook alerted his neighbors and the manhunt began. (B) Farm people searched the fields by lamplight and found a trail that led to the foothills. (C) The next morning, Jones brazenly walked into a farmer's kitchen and demanded breakfast. (D) Afterwards, he retreated to a hideout in the rock formations near Tomato Springs, the place that gave the bandit his name. (E) A posse of over 200 armed farmers and two sheriff's deputies took on the bandit in a mid-morning shoot-out. When the gun smoke cleared, Deputy Robert Squires was dead, the first Orange County law officer killed in the line of duty. (F) Jones was also dead, of a suspected self-inflicted shot. Three others were injured, including Fred "Humpy" Culver's brother Willard, who lost his leg at the knee. After the Tomato Springs saga, Willard Culver was known as "Gimpy." (Courtesy Jim Sleeper.)

CITRUS PLANTED. 1906 marked the first year of full-scale citrus planting on the Irvine Ranch. Irvine formed the San Joaquin Fruit and Investment Company with C.E. Utt and Sherman Stevens, of Tustin. The group planted 400 acres of lemons and Valencia oranges and 600 acres of walnuts and apricots. The property makes up part of the present-day village of Northwood. Until the groves matured, other dry crops were grown between the trees (Courtesy Bowers Museum, Santa Ana, California.)

PICKING ORANGES IN THE GROVES. With a dependable water supply now available, citrus production flourished. As citrus groves expanded, there was a corresponding reduction in field crop acreage. Lowlands were drained, and land that was previously used for cattle and sheep-grazing was cultivated. Irvine reinvested his profits into improved irrigation and water-conservation reservoirs. (Courtesy Bowers Museum, Santa Ana, California.)

**FRANCES PACKING HOUSE, BUILT IN 1916.** The orange groves were so bountiful that a 48,000-square-foot packinghouse was built to process the fruit. The packinghouse was located at the intersection of Shop Road (now Yale Avenue) and the Santa Fe Railway's Venta Spur. It was named for Irvine's late wife, Frances. Oranges grown by the San Joaquin Fruit Company were cleaned and labeled at the Frances Packing House and shipped around the world.

**INTERIOR OF THE FRANCES PACKING HOUSE.** While the exterior of the packinghouse was simple, the interior displayed superior architectural design. The packinghouse was unique, with high ceilings and numerous windows that gave the workspace a feeling of open space and light. The design was honored years later, when the Frances Packing House was added to the National Register of Historic Places.


63

**JAMES IRVINE SR.** Irvine lived through many changes after inheriting the Irvine Ranch in 1895. He started a family and a company and oversaw the growth and direction of both. He weathered drought, legal challenges, and the loss of his great love. But instead of weakening his resolve, Irvine's experiences made him even more committed to the land. James Felton writes that Irvine's discipline was legendary; he hated to waste time and neither smoked nor drank because "they muddied a man's thinking." Like many important men, Irvine had more critics than friends. The responsibility of his position kept Irvine from the ease of casual acquaintances.

**IRVINE WITH HIS CHILDREN, C. 1915.** By all accounts, Irvine was deeply devoted to his family. All three of his children showed potential for success, but each would endure tragedy that kept him or her from achieving it. Pictured, from left to right, are Myford, Jase, Kathryn, and James Irvine.

**JAMES IRVINE AND GLENN MARTIN, 1913.** Irvine (left) was also driven by his adventurous spirit. He went for a ride in Glenn Martin's "flying birdcage" airplane, rode camels in Egypt, and fished for trout in Chile. But no matter how far away he travelled, he never forgot the ranch for long. Wherever he went, he brought back seeds and plants to test at the ranch.

JAMES "JASE" IRVINE, C. 1917. When the United States entered World War I, Jase Irvine went to Camp Lewis in Tacoma, Washington, for military training. Ralph Mitchell, son of former ranch manager Willis Mitchell, went with him. In an oral history for California State University, Fullerton, Mitchell remembered, "They were developing the camp and we had to sleep in pup tents . . . it was wet and damp and Jimmy came down with pneumonia . . . They had to send him home on the train." The illness aggravated a childhood exposure to tuberculosis, placing the Irvine heir's life in jeopardy. (Courtesy Katie Wheeler Library.)

KATHRYN HELENA MARRIES, 1919. The decade ended in celebration when Kathryn married ex-Navy flyer Frank Lillard in the teahouse on the front lawn. Pictured here are, from left to right, Jase's wife of five years, Madeline; Myford; Kathryn Helena; and her new husband, Frank. The young couple's happiness was short-lived, however, and their married life lasted less than a year. (Courtesy Katie Wheeler Library.)

# Four

# PROSPERITY MIXED WITH TRAGEDY

James Irvine Sr. was a man of great discipline and determination, who believed that sharp focus and hard work could solve any problem. When there was a problem, he would fix it. When he needed water for irrigation, he found a way to access it. Irvine ran his ranch like a sea captain, making sure that each leased farm was maintained in shipshape condition. He dictated what crops to grow and how to grow them. And during his 55 years at the helm, the Irvine Ranch prospered under his stewardship.

Yet, his watchful eye and close management could not prevent change from coming to the Irvine Ranch. He could not protect his family from the tragic illness and premature death that would claim more of his loved ones. He could not stop the economic pain of the Depression, although he did his best to help ease the strain on his farmers. Finally, he could not keep the US government from taking his best bean fields to build military bases at the start of World War II. This final change altered the Irvine Ranch forever, effectively ending its agricultural dominance.

As a safeguard for the future, Irvine set up the James Irvine Foundation in 1935. The foundation is a charitable organization that was designed to have controlling stock in the Irvine Company. After Irvine's death in 1947, the foundation became the majority stockholder. The James Irvine Foundation's purpose was to fund needy causes, but it was also created to ensure that the family's agricultural empire would stay in one piece. Even though the foundation was meant to preserve the status quo, change inevitably found its way to the Irvine Ranch.

**KATHRYN HELENA IRVINE LILLARD (1897–1920).** For the Irvine family, the decade began with joyous celebration followed by tragic loss. After her marriage to Frank Lillard, Kathryn gave birth to a daughter, Kathryn Anita. The blessing of James Irvine's first grandchild came with a cost. Weakened by pneumonia, Kathryn Helena died days after childbirth. (Courtesy Orange County Archives.)

**KATHRYN ANITA "KATIE" LILLARD, BORN 1920.** Kathryn Anita, known as "Katie," was a delightful addition to the Irvine household, even with the sad circumstances of her birth. Years later, when an exact replica of the Irvine family home was constructed for use as a library, it was named the Katie Wheeler Library after the little girl who grew up there. (Courtesy Katie Wheeler Library.)

**JAMES IRVINE AND KATIE, C. 1922.** Suddenly, the stoic and serious Irvine was faced with the challenge of raising a little girl. Years later, in an interview, Katie Wheeler explained her grandfather's personality: "He lived alone for so long that he did things his own way. He was a good guy, and a self-made man with great vision. I was in awe of him when I was very, very young." (Courtesy Katie Wheeler Library.)

**BRAD HELLIS, C. 1920.** Brad Hellis was a neighborhood friend of the Irvine children when they lived in San Francisco. Later, at the age of 22, he came to work at the Irvine Ranch. Living in an apartment next to Irvine's office, Hellis worked his way up from running errands to ranch manager. A trusted employee and frequent hunting companion, Hellis was an important figure on the Irvine Ranch for 45 years. (Courtesy First American Corporation.)

**FIELD MANAGER WITH IRVINE COMPANY CROP.** The farm lease agreement required tenants to give a percentage of their crop to the Irvine Company. One of Hellis's earliest jobs as a field manager was counting the sacks of barley and beans to make sure that the company received its proper share. The tenant farmers gave Hellis the nickname "Count du Sack."

**EDDIE MARTIN.** Eddie Martin (no relation to the pioneering pilot Glenn) was an entrepreneurial aviator who leased 80 acres on the Irvine Ranch for his airport. In Leslie Berkman's *The Irvine Saga*, Martin recalls that when he could not afford to pay his rent during the Depression, Irvine tore up the agreement and said, "We'll just do business by handshake." Martin offered plane rides for $10 and, at his flight school, taught many local residents how to fly.

**EDDIE MARTIN AIRPORT, 1933.** The Eddie Martin Airport was located at the intersection of South Main Street and Newport Boulevard. Today, the location would be at the intersection of the 55 Freeway and Main Street. This image, looking south, shows crowds arriving for one of Martin's popular air shows. Main Street is at the bottom of the picture, intersecting with Newport Boulevard, which runs diagonally. In 1939, the airport was closed, and Martin's operations were moved southwest to the new Orange County Airport.

**TRAFFIC IN IRVINE, C. 1928.** The intersection in the middle of Irvine—where Laguna Road, Central Avenue, and the Santa Fe railroad met—was notoriously dangerous. There were no railroad crossing gates or stoplights, and a billboard advertising Laguna Beach created a blind spot. Many crashes occurred at the intersection and, in 1929, after a wealthy car dealer from Los Angeles was killed, Laguna Road was realigned to the north side of town, near the present-day Interstate 5. (Courtesy Orange County Archives.)

**NEW SCHOOL, BUILT IN 1929.** Irvine Ranch children received a new school in 1929, located just northeast of town on Central Avenue (now Sand Canyon Avenue). The original school building was turned into a community center and was used for meetings and monthly dances. Before the El Camino and College Park schools were built in 1973, students rode buses to the 1929 school building for class.

**AERIAL VIEW OF IRVINE.** After the realignment of Laguna Road, a new street, Burt Lane, was created. The Irvine Service Station was moved to the corner of the new road and Central, now Sand Canyon, Avenue, which runs horizontally across the image above. Just south of the service station was the Irvine Café, where travelers could stop for "the best burgers, beans and black coffee." The house facing Central Avenue was the home of George Cook, who leased the largest lima bean field on the ranch. In 1990, Cook's house was relocated to the San Joaquin Marsh and Wildlife Sanctuary.

**IRVINE SERVICE STATION.** To meet growing demand, the Irvine Service Station had six gas pumps. Gasoline was pumped up into the glass chambers at the top and then released into the auto tank by gravity. Former Irvine farmer George Veeh remembers that the employees "worked hard to put the 'service' in the service station." The man pictured is unidentified.

IRVINE COFFEE SHOP. The coffee shop was the social center of the town. Farmers came in every day for a cup of coffee and the latest news. Each farmer had his own coffee mug waiting for him on the shelf. On rainy days, some would stay and play the few slot machines that were in the back room, but when the local sheriff found out, the slot machines soon disappeared.

IRVINE COFFEE SHOP INTERIOR. Proprietor Henry Sizer served a 35¢ luncheon special every day. According to the *Rancho San Joaquin Gazette*, the coffee shop had a reputation for having "the best food for miles around," which attracted loyal customers who came "even if they didn't know what they were going to get."

**IRVINE STORE.** The center of activity was still the Irvine Store, a Red & White store, where townspeople would go to get their mail from one of the 92 brass post office boxes or use one of the only phones on the ranch. Kate Munger's two brothers, Horace, and, later, Boyd, managed the Irvine Store until 1946.

**BEAN PICKERS, 1939.** A new bean-picking room was built on the second floor of the 1895 warehouse. Forty-eight women worked at six tables, studying beans moving past them on conveyor belts. The women picked out any cracked or broken beans and removed any remaining dirt or stems. After long hours on a bean-picking shift, many workers complained of dizziness.

**ALBERT A. MICHELSON, ALBERT EINSTEIN, ROBERT MILLIKAN, 1931.** Nobel Prize–winning physicist Albert Michelson came to the Irvine Ranch to measure the speed of light. In 1929, Michelson met with James Irvine, who agreed to lease him land in a flat bean field at the north end of the ranch. The experiment was conducted parallel to the present-day Armstrong Avenue, from McGaw Avenue to Barranca Parkway. Pictured, from left to right, are (first row) Albert Michelson, Albert Einstein, and Robert Millikan; (second row) Walter S. Adams, Walther Mayer, and Max Ferrand. (Courtesy Smithsonian Institution Libraries.)

**MICHELSON'S SPEED OF LIGHT EXPERIMENT, 1930.** The experiment design included a metal shack, which contained turbines and the arc light that would be measured. The scientists built a mile-long airtight tube, three feet in diameter, which extended from the shack. The result was one of the most recognized measurements in physics—the speed of light. Michelson passed away in 1931, unable to see the final publication of his findings. (Courtesy California Institute of Technology.)

**WESTERN SALT COMPANY, ESTABLISHED 1949.** Another innovative use of ranch land operated in the Back Bay. Oscar Huffine leased 250 acres from Irvine and built a series of settling ponds for the purpose of "farming" salt. The Western Salt Company took over the saltworks lease in 1949 and produced about 7,000 tons of salt per year. Most of it was sold to laundries or used for water softeners.

**BACK BAY SALT WORKS, BUILT IN 1934.** Ocean water from the bay was trapped and moved slowly through a series of ponds. The sun evaporated the salt water, reducing it to heavy brine and eventually forming crystals. The crystals were loaded onto a narrow gauge railway and taken to a two-story mill to be cleaned and prepared for sale. The saltworks, located near Jamboree Road, was damaged in a severe rainstorm and later demolished in 1969.

**SANTIAGO CANYON DAM RESERVOIR, IRVINE LAKE, 1939.** The Irvine Ranch had over 2,500 deepwater wells, but when the water table dropped, a new dependable water supply was needed. Irvine built a series of dams and water-conservation reservoirs to solve the problem. The reservoirs collected runoff water from the Santiago Mountains to be used for irrigation. The Santiago Reservoir, also known as Irvine Lake, was built in 1931 and was the largest reservoir in the system.

**HIGH LINE CANAL.** In order to bring the stored water from the reservoirs down to the ranch, Irvine built the 22-mile, granite High Line Canal. Water flowed to the fields by the force of gravity. Gates were used to control the direction of the water flow. (Courtesy First American Corporation.)

THE CITRUS GROVES MATURE. In order to protect the orchards from the fierce Santa Ana winds, eucalyptus trees were planted as windbreaks. The trees were planted close together in straight rows, 250 trees to the mile. (Courtesy Bowers Museum, Santa Ana, California.)

TUBERCULOSIS HEALTH CAMP, 1926. The Orange County Tuberculosis Association built The Preventorium, a 10-acre health camp, near Irvine Regional Park. James Irvine donated the land. The purpose was to build up "sickly" children with exercise and fresh air to ward off the "white plague" of tuberculosis. The camp closed during the Depression, in 1932, due to a lack of funding. Ironically, the Irvine family would soon experience the tragedy of tuberculosis firsthand. (Courtesy First American Corporation.)

**ATHALIE RICHARDSON IRVINE, 1929.** After a 12-year marriage to Madeline Agassiz ended in divorce, Jase Irvine married Athalie Richardson in 1929. The newlyweds moved into the Irvine family home at the ranch headquarters compound. Athalie enjoyed the company of her new father-in-law and was amazed at his ability to describe the origin of every tree growing on the ranch. (Courtesy Katie Wheeler Library.)

**KATHARINE WHITE IRVINE.** Soon after his eldest son married, James H. Irvine followed suit. After 22 years as a widower, he married San Francisco philanthropist Katharine White in 1931. The formidable woman was an equal match, in both personality and presence, for the strong-willed Irvine. Katharine White Irvine, known as "Big Kate," was known for her big hats and her eight small Pekingese dogs. She is pictured with her husband's hunting dogs.

ATHALIE ANITA "JOAN" IRVINE. In 1933, Athalie and Jase Irvine had their only child—a daughter they named Athalie Anita, after her mother and her grandmother. A pretty and precocious little girl, Athalie Anita requested that her name be changed to Joan, after a favorite nursery rhyme. Her request was granted, and she was known as Joan from then on.

JAMES H. IRVINE JR. (1893–1935). From the time he was a boy, Jase Irvine was groomed to take over the Irvine Ranch. He learned every aspect of the operation, from the front office to the fields, in preparation for his future job as head of the Irvine Company. But illness kept him from succeeding his father as planned. Even though great effort was made to rehabilitate him, Irvine Jr. died in 1935 after surgery to treat his tuberculosis. He was 42 years old.

**JAMES H. IRVINE SR.** Jase Irvine's untimely death radically changed Irvine Sr.'s plans for the future of his company. In 1937, J.I. set up the James Irvine Foundation, eventually transferring the majority of Irvine Company stock to the charitable organization. The purpose of the foundation was both philanthropic and practical. Irvine wanted his landholdings to remain intact, and he believed that the foundation, guided by his own handpicked advisors, would ensure that his wishes were followed.

**IRVINE FAMILY CHRISTMAS CARD, 1939.** Every year, James Irvine insisted on creating the annual Christmas card himself, often including his own brave attempts at poetry. This card depicts the annual Fourth of July celebration at Irvine Cove, the family's house near Laguna Beach.

KATE

THE FRIENDS

Merry Christmas
AND
Happy New Year

JAMES AND KATHARINE IRVINE

JULY 4, 1939

GRANDPA

THE FUN

THE SPOT

**CHRISTMAS DINNER FOR THE FIVE-YEAR CLUB.** Irvine Company employees of five years or more were invited to the annual Christmas dinner at the ranch headquarters mess hall. After dinner, Irvine, seated at the back table, would get up and say a few words. Then, the guests would politely watch movies from his latest travels.

**MYFORD IRVINE, KATIE WHEELER, AND CHARLES WHEELER.** J.I.'s granddaughter Katie married Charles Wheeler in 1941. A well-liked couple, Charlie managed the ranch operations from 1953 to 1977, and Katie was the longest-serving member on the James Irvine Foundation board.

IRVINE VALENCIA GROWERS' "SATIN" ORANGE-CRATE LABEL. The Valencia orange is a hybrid that was created by William Wolfskill, an early California pioneer. In 1866, Wolfskill sold his land and the hybrid to Irvine, whose ranch would become one of the world's largest Valencia orange producers. Known as "the king of the juice oranges," Valencias are a sweet fruit that produces a bright, orange-colored juice.

IRVINE CITRUS ASSOCIATION. Due to increased lemon production, the Irvine Citrus Association was formed and took over an old lemon facility next to the Frances Packing House. The two plants were connected by a conveyor belt and the precooling plant was shared between them. The peak season for the Irvine Citrus Association was 1937, when over 1,246 railcar loads of lemons were shipped. (Courtesy First American Corporation.)

**IRVINE VALENCIA GROWERS.** Increased orange acreage required a third citrus association and an additional packinghouse on the Irvine Ranch. The Irvine Valencia Growers built a processing facility in 1929 on Jeffrey Road, near Irvine Boulevard. The Santa Fe Venta spur was extended to reach the new facility and was named Kathryn, in honor of James Irvine's late daughter. In 1938, the members of IVG controlled more than 3,800 acres of Valencia oranges groves. By 1969, acreage had nearly doubled, to 6,338.

**VALENCIA ORANGE PROCESSING.** The Irvine Valencia Growers Association gathered the handpicked oranges from the orchards and transported them to the packinghouse. There, they were cleaned, rated for quality, and then packed for shipment on the Santa Fe line. The Sunkist Company marketed and sold the oranges, placing its label on the highest-quality fruit.

**IRVINE FAMILY CHRISTMAS CARD, 1942.** The advent of World War II brought a revolutionary change to the Irvine Ranch. The Navy selected a site in the middle of Irvine's most productive bean field to build a military base. Irvine did not want to sell his land and presented other sites that he offered to lease free of charge. The government refused and purchased two prime fields, constructing the El Toro Marine Corps Air Station and Naval Air Station Santa Ana.

**LIGHTER-THAN-AIR BASE, 1942.** The Navy purchased 1,200 acres to build Naval Air Station Santa Ana and quickly began to construct the 17-story blimp hangars that became Orange County landmarks. The first of two wooden-frame hangars was completed in a mere nine months. (Courtesy First American Corporation.)

**BLIMP HANGAR INTERIOR, C. 1942.** Seven K-Class blimps could be stored inside the massive hangars at one time. The 250-foot-long blimps were used for coastal antisubmarine surveillance and carried crews of 10. The blimps were also armed for warfare, stocked with four depth bombs and a .50-caliber machine gun. (Courtesy Tustin Area Historical Society.)

**SHEEP GRAZING NEAR NAS SANTA ANA.** The blimp hangars were two of the largest wooden structures ever built, at a cost of $2 million each. The iconic Orange County landmarks were built on land that was once an alfalfa farm. The base was later converted to a Marine Corps helicopter training facility. (Courtesy First American Corporation.)

**EL TORO MARINE BASE, EST. 1943.** The wide-open space of Irvine's lima bean field was an ideal location for the home of Marine Corps aviation on the West Coast. The base's four runways were built to handle the largest aircraft in the US military inventory. (Courtesy First American Corporation.)

**T.SGT. BOB BLANKMAN, 1943.** Longtime Orange County resident Bob Blankman (left) first came to the El Toro Marine base in 1942. His division was charged with preparing the base for the squadron of dive-bombers and fighter planes that would be stationed there. Blankman found the local climate preferable to that of his native state of New York and, like many enlisted men at El Toro, he eventually settled in California. (Courtesy First American Corporation.)

**EL TORO MARINE BASE DEDICATION CEREMONY, 1943.** During the base dedication ceremony, a planned flyover of dive-bombers and wildcat fighters ended in tragedy. A pilot of a wildcat fighter was unable to pull out of a barrel roll maneuver and crashed his plane as horrified dignitaries looked on. (Courtesy First American Corporation.)

**AERIAL VIEW OF EL TORO MARINE BASE, 1956.** The arrival of the El Toro Marine Base changed the Irvine Ranch forever. The once-sleepy bean field was replaced with active runways that launched high-speed jets across the countryside. (Courtesy of First American Corporation.)

**James H. Irvine Dies, 1947.** Irvine used the funds from the Navy to purchase the 82,000-acre Flying D Ranch in Bozeman, Montana. On August 24, 1947, just two months before his 80th birthday, James Harvey Irvine Sr. died of a heart attack while fishing in a stream on his Montana ranch. Athalie Clark remembered her former father-in-law as "a great, great lover of land. I think the money was secondary. It was the great expanse of land that he loved and cherished." Irvine passionately guarded his beloved California ranch for 55 years. With his death, an era came to an end. But even a visionary like James Irvine could not imagine the changes that were to come.

# Five

# CULTIVATING COMMUNITIES

Myford Irvine was not a farmer. His older brother, Jase, had been groomed to be the logical successor to their father's control of an agricultural empire. Myford spent most of his adult life managing the family's financial interests in San Francisco. So, when his brother's untimely death placed Myford next in line to control the Irvine Company, it was no surprise that his development interests were more residential than agricultural.

Myford Irvine believed that the value of land lay not only in the cultivation of crops but also for the enjoyment of people, who were moving to Orange County in droves during the postwar population boom. In 1953, Irvine spent $250,000 to host the weeklong Boy Scout Jamboree. He developed beautiful coastline communities in Newport and Laguna Beach, wanting to create a "Beverly Hills of Orange County." Finally, he was in favor of bringing a University of California campus to the Irvine Ranch.

Unfortunately, he would never see the university he had supported. In 1959, Myford Irvine was found dead in the basement of the family home, the result of suicide. Even though his death generated more questions than answers, the reasons for his tragic death were buried with him. Myford Irvine was the last of his generation, and with his passing, all three of James Irvine Sr.'s children were gone.

Another family member was ready to step forward as protector of the Irvine legacy. In 1957, Myford's niece (and Jase Irvine's daughter), Joan Irvine Smith, joined the Irvine Company board of directors. Strong-willed and outspoken, Smith insisted that the company donate 1,000 acres for the University of California campus—despite the resistance of many board members. Her public persistence won out, and in the fall of 1965, the University of California, Irvine (UCI) welcomed students to the first day of classes.

The Irvine Company was so pleased with the design of the new university that it commissioned the architect, William Pereira, to design a master plan for the Irvine Ranch. In 1960, plans were set in motion to create what Irvine Company president Charles Thomas called, "the largest and most diversified land development conceived by man."

**BULK PROCESSING WAREHOUSE, BUILT IN 1949.** Shortly after Irvine Sr.'s death, the switch was made to bulk processing as a way to cut costs. Warehouse manager Bill Cook helped organize local farmers into the Irvine Bean and Grain Growers Association, which would share the expenses and the profits based on individual production. The 32 silos were each 35 feet tall and could hold a total of 16 million pounds of beans and barley. Today, the warehouse has been converted into a hotel. (Used with permission of The Irvine Company. © The Irvine Company LLC 2011. All Rights Reserved.)

**TOP VIEW OF SILO.** Beans were carried through the warehouse on conveyor belts and loaded into silos. Bean ladders were positioned inside the silos to slow the flow of beans so that they would not be broken or crushed by the time they hit the bottom. The ladders had to be placed at the proper angles to regulate the flow of beans: too slow, and they would clog the chute; too fast, and the beans would be broken and unusable.

**MYFORD IRVINE.** Following the death of James Irvine Sr., in 1947, his only remaining child became president of the Irvine Company. Myford Irvine, known as Mike, spent most of his adult life in San Francisco. Since he was unfamiliar with agricultural operations, he turned his focus to coastal residential development and relied on Brad Hellis to manage the ranch. Myford led the Irvine Company's residential projects at Harbor View Hills, Dover Shores, and Irvine Terrace, all in Newport Beach.

**MYFORD AND GLORIA WHITE IRVINE WEDDING, 1950.** Myford Irvine married his second wife, Gloria Wood White, in 1950. The couple created a blended family with their children Linda Jane Irvine, Bill White, and Gay White. In 1953, they had a son, James Myford Irvine. Gloria White Irvine was previously married to William White II, son of James Irvine Sr.'s second wife, Katharine. (Courtesy Katie Wheeler Library.)

**BOY SCOUT JAMBOREE TRAIN FLYER, 1953.** One of Myford Irvine's first orders of business was to work with Irvine Company vice president Bill Spurgeon to host the national Boy Scout Jamboree. Over 50,000 Boy Scouts came from across the nation, many on specially designated railcars that stopped at landmarks, such as the Grand Canyon, along the way. (Used with permission of The Irvine Company. © The Irvine Company LLC 2011. All Rights Reserved.)

**AERIAL VIEW OF THE BOY SCOUT JAMBOREE, 1953.** The Irvine Company cleared land and leveled hills in preparation for the jamboree. An eight-mile road, later named Jamboree, was graded to access the camp of 35,000 tents that covered what are now the Newport Center and East Bluff neighborhoods. Telephone and electrical service were installed, and 88 miles of pipe were laid for the water supply. "Jamboree Town" had its own fire station, police force, medical facility, and post office. (Courtesy Orange County Archives.)

**VICE PRES. RICHARD NIXON ADDRESSES SCOUTS, 1953.** Vice President Nixon, a former Boy Scout from Whittier, California, camped overnight at the jamboree. After making pancakes with the boys, he addressed the assembled Scouts at an afternoon convocation in the 75,000-seat amphitheater. (Courtesy Orange County Archives.)

**ORANGE COUNTY BOY SCOUTS AT JAMBOREE, 1953.** The Irvine Ranch formed its own Boy Scout Troop 36 to host the festivities. Jamboree Road extended from the Troop 36 clubhouse, at the ranch headquarters, all the way to the jamboree site. Many of the Scouts in Troop 36 were sons of ranch workers, including Myford Irvine's stepson, Bill White, pictured here in the second row, fourth from the right. (Courtesy William White.)

**JAMBOREE TOWN, 1953.** The Scouts cooked their own food over charcoal fires. They consumed over 200,000 pounds of meat, 500,000 eggs, and 169,594 loaves of bread. For dessert, they ate 62,800 pies and washed them down with 623,656 quarts of milk. When they were not cooking or eating, the Scouts were busy trading hometown artifacts with other Scouts. Dr. Dennis Mull, a former UCI professor who attended the jamboree, took the horn of a Texas longhorn home with him on the train. (Courtesy Orange County Archives.)

**AERIAL VIEW OF FASHION ISLAND.** The infrastructure built for the jamboree laid the foundation for more development on the Irvine Ranch. The pipelines that were put down for the Boy Scouts were later used for Myford Irvine's public golf course, the Irvine Coast Country Club. Jamboree Town later became Newport Center and Fashion Island.

**MYFORD IRVINE AT BUFFALO RANCH, 1955.**
During the same year that Disneyland
opened its gates, 100 bison were shipped
from Kansas to create the Newport
Harbor Buffalo Ranch. Although not as
famous as the Magic Kingdom, the Buffalo
Ranch was a popular tourist attraction.
Located at the present-day corner of
Bonita Canyon Road and MacArthur
Boulevard, it was the first commercial
lease offered to an outside business on
the Irvine Ranch. Today, a bison statue
marks the location of the buffalo ranch.

**NEWPORT HARBOR BUFFALO RANCH,
1955.** The buffalo ranch offered a taste
of the Old West, with buffalo burgers,
a petting zoo, and even a real Apache
chief—Geronimo's grandson Chief
Kuthle Geronimo III. In this promotional
photograph, T. Texas Tiny (center), a 400-
pound radio disc jockey, enjoys a custom-
made buffalo burger while owner Gene
Clark (right) and an unidentified man look
on. (Courtesy Orange County Parks.)

**CATTLE OPERATION ON IRVINE RANCH.** Long before lima beans and Valencia oranges, cattle populated the Irvine Ranch. The cattle operations were located in the old 1864 San Joaquin Ranch house, next to the present-day golf course. By the 1960s, there were as many as 4,000 head of cattle, making the Irvine Ranch the largest cattle ranch in Orange County.

**SPRING ROUNDUP, BOMMER CANYON.** Every spring, the Irvine Ranch cowboys would ride out all across the ranch to round up the herd. All of the Orange County ranches pitched in to help each other, sharing their cowboys to tackle the job. After the hard work was over, there was a great roundup barbecue at the cattle camp in Bommer Canyon. (Used with permission of The Irvine Company. © The Irvine Company LLC 2011. All Rights Reserved.)

**ROPING A CALF AT THE ROUNDUP.**
Once the herd was gathered at
Bommer Canyon, the cowboys
roped the calves for branding. In
this photograph, Bill White lassos a
running calf at the spring roundup.
(Courtesy William White.)

**BRANDING AND CUTTING IN 1982.**
The cowboys worked in precision
teams and were able to rope, brand,
castrate, and inoculate a calf in less
than one minute. In this picture,
cowboy Ron Rodriguez (left) prepares
to brand, after ranch manager Bob
Elder (right) finishes castrating the
calf. Bill White (center) looks on.

**BOB ELDER.** The cowboy's job was to monitor and care for the herd year-round. A good cowboy learned to "think like a cow," using years of experience and observation to stay one step ahead of the herd. Bob Elder, who was head of cattle operations in the final years in the 1980s, told the Irvine Historical Society, "The Irvine cowboy is a cut above the average." (Courtesy William White.)

**RAY SERRANO AND PHIL CROSTHWAITE.** Ray Serrano (left) and Phil Crosthwaite (right) descended from a long line of local cowboys whose families dated back to the Spanish rancho era. Even though modern technology had changed the cowboy's job, Crosthwaite and Serrano cared for the herd as the vaqueros had for generations. They are pictured here with Joe Gomez.

**CHARLIE WHEELER'S VIEW OF THE IRVINE RANCH.** Charlie Wheeler managed ranch operations from 1953 to 1977. Residential development took Orange County by storm in the 1960s, but cattle were still able to roam the open spaces of the Irvine Ranch. Development finally ended the era of the cattle ranch, and the last of the herd was rounded up at Bommer Canyon in 1985. (Courtesy William White.)

**HORSE PADDOCK NEAR TURTLE ROCK.** In the mid-1960s, the cattle ranch camp moved from the San Joaquin Ranch House to Bommer Canyon. A paddock for the ranch horses was located nearby, in the present-day neighborhood of Turtle Rock. Currently, the paddock building is used as the Turtle Rock Nature Center. (Used with permission of The Irvine Company. © The Irvine Company LLC 2011. All Rights Reserved.)

GLORIA IRVINE AND CHILDREN, 1950S. Horses were a big part of the Irvine family tradition, and this love of riding was passed on to Myford's children. The ranch was a kid's paradise in the 1950s, providing the Irvine children and their friends with an ideal place to grow up.

GLORIA IRVINE IN FAMILY CAR. The Irvine ranch house was again full of family. Gloria is at the wheel, and seated in the back of the car are, from left to right, Linda Irvine, Gay White, and Bill White. The Newport Harbor residential island of Linda Isle was named for Myford Irvine's daughter, Linda. (Courtesy Katie Wheeler Library.)

**JOAN IRVINE SMITH AND HER MOTHER, ATHALIE IRVINE CLARKE.** In 1957, when she was 24 years old, Joan Irvine Smith took her mother's position on The Irvine Company board of directors. Strong-willed like her grandfather, Joan Irvine Smith was a formidable member of the board who vigorously debated the direction of The Irvine Company in an effort to preserve her family's legacy. (Courtesy Katie Wheeler Library.)

**MYFORD PLUM IRVINE (1898–1959).** On January 11, 1959, Myford Irvine was found dead in the basement of the family home. Although it was controversial, the cause of death was ruled to be suicide. After Myford Irvine's untimely death, an Irvine family member would never again serve as president of the Irvine Company.

**WILLIAM PEREIRA, PLANNER.** When the decision was made to build a University of California campus on the Irvine Ranch, noted architect William Pereira was hired to develop the plan. Some of Pereira's other projects included the Los Angeles International Airport and the Transamerica Building in San Francisco.

**UNIVERSITY OF CALIFORNIA, IRVINE, MASTER PLAN.** In 1961, Pereira set up his planning operation at the old Buffalo Ranch and renamed it "Urbanus Square." Using a renovated red barn as the central office, Pereira and his staff produced the plans for the UCI campus, as well as Newport Center. Pictured in this image are, from left to right, UCI chancellor Daniel Aldrich, Pereira, and Irvine Company president Charles Thomas. (Used with permission of The Irvine Company. © The Irvine Company LLC 2011. All Rights Reserved.)

UCI Before Construction. The regents of the University of California system were not convinced that the Irvine Ranch site was ideal for their new campus; they feared the location was too remote. However, the expansive ranch land offered room to grow in the future. In 1960, the Irvine Company donated 1,000 acres and sold an additional 500 acres to the University of California. (Courtesy City of Irvine.)

Aerial View of UCI, 1960s. Pereira's design for the campus was wheel-shaped, with six academic quadrangles surrounding a 16-acre central park that was intended to be the focus of university life. The advantage of circular design was that major academic buildings and athletic facilities would all be within a 10-minute walk of each other. In a 1965 article in *Orange County Illustrated* magazine, Pereira explains his belief that "parks and other open spaces restore the land to the pedestrian. These open spaces must be connected by a pedestrian way." (Used with permission of The Irvine Company. © The Irvine Company LLC 2011. All Rights Reserved.)

**UCI, 1960s.** The university was intended to be the heart of the new community that would soon surround it. Pereira also says in the article that "the 'starfish shape' of the campus will allow the university to penetrate into the surrounding community, drawing strength from it and infusing it with intellectual vitality." (Courtesy Orange County Archives.)

**UCI DEDICATION CEREMONY, 1964.** Pres. Lyndon B. Johnson gave the dedication address at the new university on June 20, 1964. He concluded his speech with the words, "In education, in health, in transportation . . . let us move forward to do our best, knowing that 'whatsoever man soweth, that shall he also reap.'" (Courtesy City of Irvine.)

**UCI, 1965.** Five years after William Pereira was hired to design the new campus, classes began for over 1,500 students in September 1965. In *Orange County Illustrated*, chancellor Daniel Aldrich, who had an extensive background in agricultural research, used an appropriate analogy to describe the new university on the Irvine Ranch: "The soil is right for excellent academic crops." (Courtesy City of Irvine.)

**UCI's Peter the Anteater.** When university administrators sought ideas for a new school mascot, a group of irreverent students proposed the anteater. The idea for an anteater mascot was inspired by the anteater in Johnny Hart's comic strip, B.C. At first, Peter the Anteater was not well received by members of the campus administration, who felt it was too undignified to represent the campus. But the student body and their chants of "Zot, Zot, Zot!" prevailed. (Courtesy City of Irvine.)

**OPEN SPACE, C. 1964.** The UCI master plan called for no walls, visible or invisible, in Irvine. It was purposely planted in the center of the future community. This early image of the campus shows the undeveloped hills in the background, before the existence of the communities of Turtle Rock and University Park. In this image, the El Toro Marine Base can be seen beneath Saddleback Mountain, and Turtle Rock can be seen on the hillside behind the campus. (Courtesy City of Irvine.)

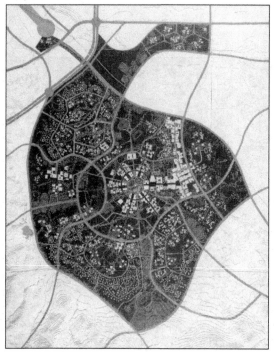

**IRVINE MASTER PLAN.** After UCI was completed, Pereira shifted his attention to developing the master plan for the city that would surround it. In a September 1963 *Time* magazine article, he states, "In recent years, we here in California have become rather expert at abusing our land and our resources. Here we have a tremendous opportunity to point people's tastes and expectations in another direction. And we can do it—the sheer size of the place makes almost anything possible." (Courtesy City of Irvine.)

# Six

# THE NEW TOWN

In 1960, William Pereira was presented with unprecedented opportunity. Never before had a planning and architectural firm been entrusted with the responsibility of not only designing a major university, but master-planning the entire community of which it would be a part. The concept of the new town—a residential environment containing all of the elements needed for its citizens—was a revolutionary idea at the time. Similar communities had been created across the country with encouraging success, and Irvine was to be the largest.

The university nurtured a symbiotic relationship with the community that surrounded it, with each nourishing and supporting the growth of the other. Throughout the 1960s, the residential villages of University Park and Turtle Rock encircled the university with community-minded citizens ready to be part of their newly adopted neighborhoods. The initial phase of the Irvine master plan was a success. Soon, the entire nation would take notice.

On March 19, 1970, Irvine Company president William Mason and vice president Ray Watson announced plans for the largest planned city in the western hemisphere. The city of Irvine, comprising 53,000 acres, would be twice the size of San Francisco. It would be home to 24 separate residential villages, over 4,000 acres of industrial development, and 2,400 acres of open space for parks. But Irvine's most unique feature was not the quantity of its acreage, but the quality of life it offered. According to the *Los Angeles Times*, "The plan presents an encouraging awareness of life values to go along with property values. Its accent is not as much on size and growth as on the quality of the environment."

By 1971, Irvine had everyone's attention. Neighboring cities made plans to annex the valuable lands of unincorporated Irvine for themselves. Also, Irvine's new residents were eager to have more of a say in the direction of their community, and on December 28, 1971, Irvine citizens voted in favor of incorporation. Orange County's newest city, already rich with history, was born.

**IRVINE RANCH ANNIVERSARY OPEN HOUSE, 1964.** To mark the 100th anniversary of James Irvine's purchase of his ranch land, The Irvine Company held a public open house event. Guests took history tours of the Irvine Ranch, enjoyed a glass of orange juice at the packinghouse, and then gathered for a reception on the lawn of the former family home. The Irvine Ranch House had been converted into offices for the Irvine Company. (Courtesy Katie Wheeler Library.)

**IRVINE RANCH HOUSE FIRE, 1965.** On June 5, 1965, the Red Hill Volunteer Fire Department was called to a fire at the former Irvine family home. The damage was extensive, and the structure was eventually demolished in 1968. In 2008, a replica of the original home opened to the public as the Katie Wheeler Library. (Courtesy Katie Wheeler Library.)

**IRVINE COMPANY PLANNING TEAM.**
When Charles Thomas became
president of the Irvine Company in
1960, he assembled a team of young
planners, architects, and engineers
to implement William Pereira's
plans for the Irvine Ranch. William
Mason became vice president of
engineering, Lansing Eberling was
hired as controller, and Ray Watson
(above right, with two unidentified
members of his planning crew) was
named vice president of planning.
(Used with permission of The Irvine
Company. © The Irvine Company
LLC 2011. All Rights Reserved.)

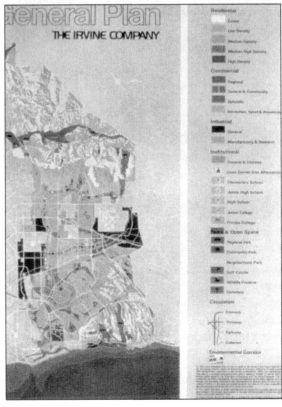

**GENERAL PLAN.** Pereira's original plan
consisted of three tiers: community
development along the 35,000-acre
coastal third of the ranch, agriculture
on the 20,000-acre central portion,
and recreation in the 33,000-acre
mountainous northern sector.

UNIVERSITY PARK, C. 1965. The master plan featured the concept of villages. Each neighborhood developed its own identity, giving residents a local community feeling within the larger development. The village of University Park was a Planned Unit Development, or PUD, which offered an all-inclusive community plan. Not only were diverse housing options available, but the plan also included commercial facilities, parks, schools, and churches. (Courtesy Orange County Archives.)

UNIVERSITY PARK UNITS, C. 1965. Even though the first 585 units in University Park were offered at an affordable price of $19,950 each, the development was not a success. There was no nearby shopping available at the time, and Interstate 405 was not yet complete. The units sold poorly, and the Irvine Company had to bail out the bankrupted builder. (Courtesy Orange County Archives.)

THE VILLAGE OF TURTLE ROCK, C. 1967. In 1967, construction began on the village of Turtle Rock, with hillside-view homes overlooking the university. In this image, Turtle Rock Drive runs across the middle of the page and intersects with Campus Drive on the right. The UCI campus is at the top of the image. (Used with permission of The Irvine Company. © The Irvine Company LLC 2011. All Rights Reserved.)

TURTLE ROCK. The Turtle Rock village was named for this distinctive rock formation that resembles a turtle sticking its head out of its shell. At first, Turtle Rock stood alone on the hillside, but it was later surrounded by development. Today, it can be seen in a community park on the aptly named Rockview Street.

**AERIAL VIEW OF THE VILLAGE OF TURTLE ROCK.** In 1968, the Irvine Company invited homebuilder Richard B. Smith to break ground for the first unit of the Broadmoor Development. This single-family home project pioneered the "zero lot line" concept, where a house is placed on the neighbor's property line. This results in one wide side yard instead of two small, useless side yards for every home. The houses also were built around shared central parks and were priced affordably from $27,000. (Used with permission of The Irvine Company. © The Irvine Company LLC 2011. All Rights Reserved.)

**THE VILLAGE OF TURTLE ROCK.** As the villages were developed, neighborhood association boards were formed to help reinforce the covenants, conditions, and restrictions (CC&Rs). The Irvine Company offered workshops that taught new homeowners how to run a successful neighborhood association. In this image, Margie Wakeham (standing) and Anne Davis Johnson pitch in to beautify their community.

**Ray Watson, 1973.** On March 19, 1970, the Irvine Company made national headlines when president William Mason and vice president Ray Watson announced plans for the largest master-planned community in the nation. The city of Irvine was projected to cover 53,000 acres and have a population of 430,000 by the year 2000. In many ways, Irvine was to be an experiment; such a large private landholding had never been available before. Watson believed that Irvine would provide "laboratory scale prototypes of modern urban development—American style." The newly planned city would set the standard for community development in the future. (Used with permission of The Irvine Company. © The Irvine Company LLC 2011. All Rights Reserved.)

CITRUS GROVES, C. 1970. Although residential development was creeping into the agricultural sector of the Irvine Ranch, neighborhoods were surrounded by citrus groves. Many early residents have fond memories of living out in the country with the smell of the orange blossoms. Walnut Boulevard cuts across the center of this image. The 5 Freeway lies just above it. A small portion of Culver Boulevard can be seen at the bottom left corner of the image.

THE MEYERS FAMILY, 1970. Robert and Doris Meyers bought their California Homes residence in 1970 for $35,000. Living out in the country was challenging for the Meyers family—the closest grocery store was the Stater Brothers market in Tustin. At night, it was so dark on Culver Drive that Robert would put his son Mike in the car and meet Doris at the 405 Freeway to guide her home after work. (Courtesy Richard and Doris Meyers.)

**CITY OF IRVINE INCORPORATION, 1971.** Neighboring cities wanted to annex the attractive tax base of Irvine's successful industrial park, and civic-minded residents wanted more involvement in the direction of their new hometown. On December 28, 1971, the people of Irvine voted in favor of incorporation, and Irvine became Orange County's newest city. (Used with permission of The Irvine Company. © The Irvine Company LLC 2011. All Rights Reserved.)

**IRVINE CITY POLITICS.** One of the first challenges facing the new city was deciding who would be in charge. Eighteen different neighborhood associations wanted to be part of the new city government. "In the long run, people will make the difference," said first city manager William Woollett, in an interview with *Orange County Illustrated*. "We must organize, coordinate and involve the people we have that seem to be ready and willing to help." (Used with permission of The Irvine Company. © The Irvine Company LLC 2011. All Rights Reserved.)

DEERFIELD SCHOOL GROUND-BREAKING CEREMONY, 1975. Quality schools have always been key to Irvine's success. As the city grew, the Irvine Company worked in conjunction with city government officials and the new Irvine Unified School District to plan and develop new school sites.

UNIVERSITY UNITED METHODIST CHURCH, 1969. The Irvine general plan allowed space for churches to be interspersed within the community. The University United Methodist Church, located on the corner of University and Culver Drives, was founded in 1969 and is the second oldest church in the city of Irvine.

**IRVINE RANCH INFORMATION CENTER.** The distinctive circular building, near the 5 Freeway and Myford Road, was the first stop for many prospective homebuyers. The Irvine Ranch Information Center displayed tiled murals that depicted local history, along with descriptions of the latest housing developments available for sale. (Used with permission of The Irvine Company. © The Irvine Company LLC 2011. All Rights Reserved.)

**RIBBON-CUTTING CEREMONY AT CULVER DRIVE, 1971.** Ribbons were being cut all over the new city of Irvine in the early 1970s. In this image, Orange County supervisor Thomas F. Riley (center) officially opens a section of Culver Drive. Main roads were intentionally made wider than necessary in anticipation of future population growth. (Courtesy Orange County Archives.)

FLUOR CORPORATION UNDER CONSTRUCTION. The iconic Fluor Corporation headquarters became a local landmark when it was built near the 405 Freeway in the late 1970s. The arrival of companies such as Fluor and Parker Hannifin demonstrated the high quality of corporations that were attracted to Irvine.

CAMPUS VALLEY RETAIL CENTER. As more and more people moved to Irvine, retail outlets began to follow. Each neighborhood retail center had to adhere to strict Irvine Company architectural guidelines so that it would blend in with the designated theme of the area.

LION COUNTRY SAFARI, 1970S. On June 16, 1970, Harry Shuster opened the Lion Country Safari tourist attraction near Moulton Parkway in Irvine. Visitors were able to experience a safari in their cars as they drove among the park's collection of wild animals. Of course, if someone drove a convertible to the park, he could rent an air-conditioned, safari-style Jeep for a nominal charge. (Courtesy Orange County Archives.)

LION COUNTRY RESIDENTS, 1970S. The most famous resident of the Lion Country Safari was an elderly, toothless lion named Frasier. The old lion became quite popular with the lionesses, and a population boom of cubs soon followed. Frasier's amorous accomplishments inspired 1972's PG-rated movie *Frasier, the Sensuous Lion*. Frasier is buried on the hillside above Wild Rivers Water Park. (Used with permission of The Irvine Company. © The Irvine Company LLC 2011. All Rights Reserved.)

**THE VILLAGE OF WOODBRIDGE, 1977.** In the 1970s, the keystone development of the Irvine Company was the village of Woodbridge. The project, originally called "Village A," was located on 1,700 flat acres in the center of Irvine, just north of the 405 Freeway. Woodbridge was designed to feature two man-made lakes and a retail center that could be accessed by pedestrian and bike paths. In this image, only the north lake of Woodbridge has been built. Culver Drive is at the bottom of this picture, and Barranca Parkway runs next to the right border of the lake. (Used with permission of The Irvine Company. © The Irvine Company LLC 2011. All Rights Reserved.)

**WOODBRIDGE SOUTH LAKE BRIDGE, 1980.**
Woodbridge was designed to contain as
many different recreational facilities as
possible. Most of these activities revolved
around the two man-made lakes in the
center of the village, each having its own
swimming lagoon for residents to enjoy.
North Lake lagoon has warmer water than
the South Lake lagoon because construction
crews hit a natural hot spring when they
were drilling for water in North Lake.

**PARKVIEW NEIGHBORHOOD HOME LOTTERY, WOODBRIDGE, 1976.** In June 1976, the first six sections
of Woodbridge homes were offered for sale, ranging in price from $58,000 to $90,000. The day
before the sale, buyers toured model homes and filled out interest cards. On the day of the sale,
10,000 interested buyers attended six lotteries for 350 available homes. All were instantly sold,
bringing national media attention to both Woodbridge and Irvine.

**NANCY AND PAT McDERMOTT WITH WOODBRIDGE HOME, 1976.** By the end of the 1970s, Irvine was associated with growing neighborhoods rather than growing crops. The population had exploded, from just over 10,000 residents in 1971 to more than 62,000 by the end of the decade.

**FISHING ON WOODBRIDGE SOUTH LAKE, 1981.** "Recreation is a key element to creating a community atmosphere," wrote former Woodbridge Village Association director Bob Figeira. "It is what draws individuals out of their homes and allows them to get to know their neighbors. When people move into Woodbridge, they buy into a lifestyle geared to open space and recreation areas that encourage a very social community."

**FRANCES PACKING HOUSE WALL MOVED TO IRVINE SAVINGS.** A few of the mementos of Irvine's past have been preserved. When the Frances Packing House was demolished in 1976, one wall was saved. In 1978, it was moved to the new Irvine Savings and Loan building in the Walnut Shopping Center on Culver Drive.

**TENANT HOUSES MOVED TO SAN JOAQUIN MARSH CAMPUS.** The Irvine Ranch Water District moved former tenant houses from the Irvine Ranch and brought them to join the former Duck Club building at its San Joaquin Marsh Campus. The buildings, which include the former warehouse manager's home, are used to host educational programs.

**DEVELOPMENT CONTINUES.** In 1977, the Irvine Company was under new ownership. After winning a bidding war with the Mobil Oil Company, a consortium of investors, including Joan Irvine Smith, paid $337.4 million dollars to purchase the Irvine Company. Among the investors was a successful Southern California homebuilder named Donald Bren. By 1983, Bren had bought out the other investors and was offering Joan Irvine Smith and her mother $88 million for their stock in the company. A lengthy legal dispute ensued. Eventually, Joan Irvine Smith sold her 11 percent share of the Irvine Company to Bren, ending the Irvine family's direct connection to the company they founded.

# Bibliography

Brigandi, Phil. *Orange County Place Names A to Z*. San Diego: Sunbelt Publications, 2006.

Brower, Martin A. *The Irvine Ranch: A Time for People*. Newport Beach, CA: Orange County Report, 1994.

Carpenter, Virginia. *Ranchos of Orange County: Chronologies of Early California*. Orange, CA: Paragon Agency, 2003.

Cleland, Robert Glass. *The Irvine Ranch*. San Marino, CA: Huntington Library Press, 1952.

Liebeck, Judy. *Irvine: A History of Innovation and Growth*. Houston: Pioneer Publications, 1990.

Pankey, Edgar. *Love of the Land: The Pankeys of Orange County*. Orange, CA: Chapman University Press, 2000.

Sleeper, Jim. *Bears to Briquets: A History of Irvine Park: 1897–1997*. Trabuco Canyon, CA: California Classics, 1987.

Smith, Joan Irvine. *A California Woman's Story*. Irvine, CA: Irvine Museum, 2006.

Visit us at
arcadiapublishing.com

CPSIA information can be obtained
at www.ICGtesting.com
Printed in the USA
LVOW04*0908201117
556993LV00012B/163/P